# Do you doodle?

Nikalas Catlow

Over 200 pictures to complete and create

Buster Books

First published in Great Britain in 2005 by Buster Books,
an imprint of Michael O'Mara Books Limited,
9 Lion Yard, Tremadoc Road,
London SW4 7NQ

A CIP catalogue record for this book is available from the British Library.

ISBN: 978-1–905158–13–3

10 9 8 7

Illustrated by Nikalas Catlow for Amy P.

Printed and bound in Singapore by Tien Wah Press

www.mombooks.com/busterbooks

Draw any idea
in your head.

# How do you feel?

# Build a house.

# Look out!

Make a puppet.

Make the genie appear.

Everyone smile!

Ants in your pants!

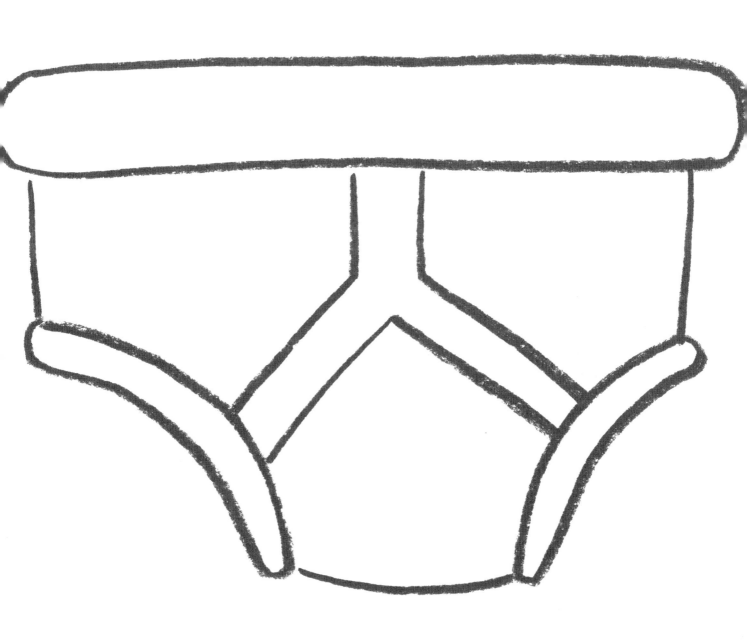

Throw the custard pies.

# Make a pile of junk.

# Which are slugs and which are snails?

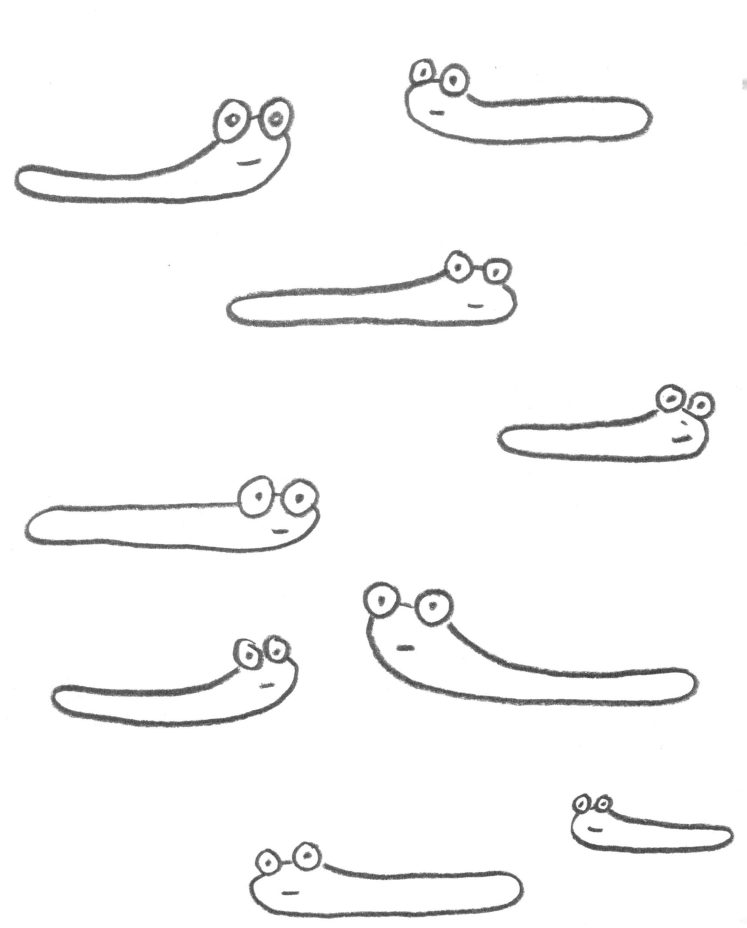

# Fantastic fireworks!

# Open the parachutes!

# Three ... Two ... One ... Liftoff!

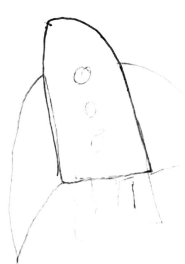

We're surrounded!

Give me the measles.

Help me escape.

Wrap me in bandages.

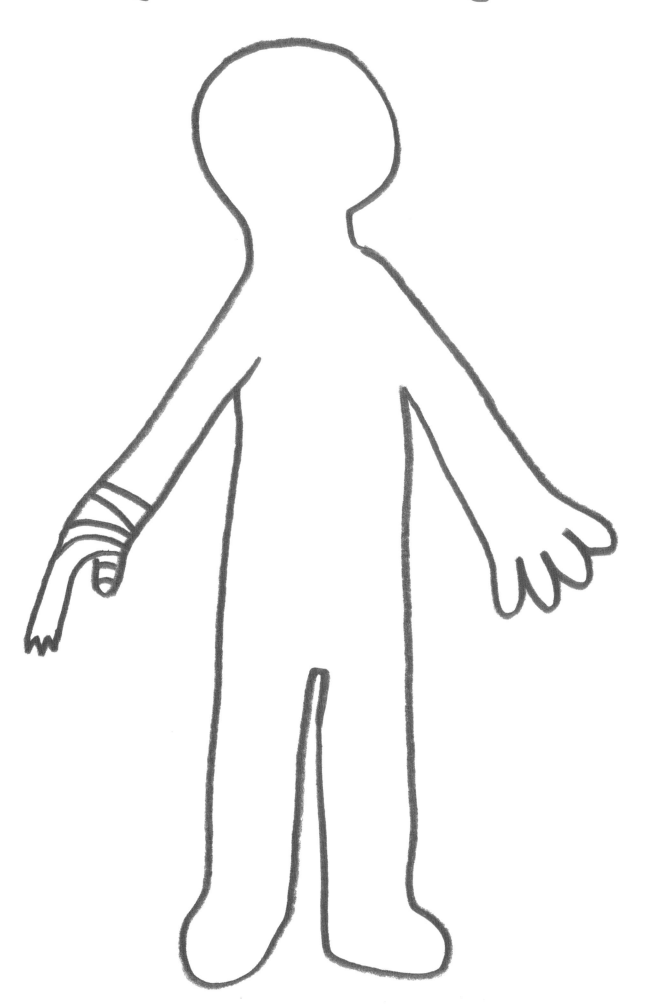

# What can you feel?

# Have a picnic.

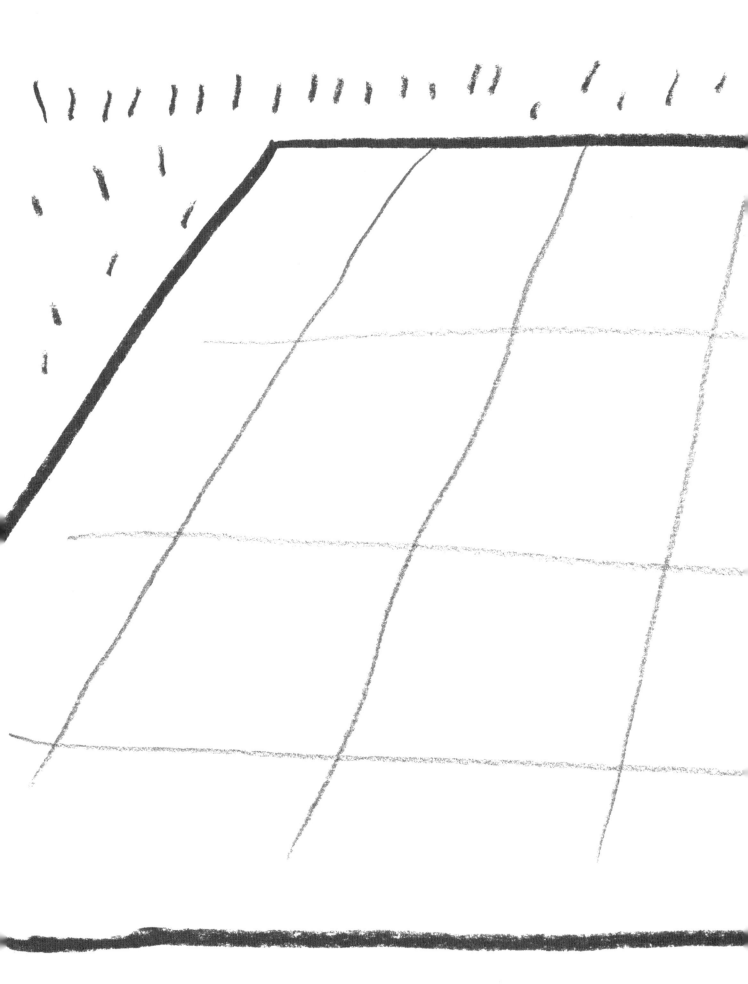

# Who's looking at whom?

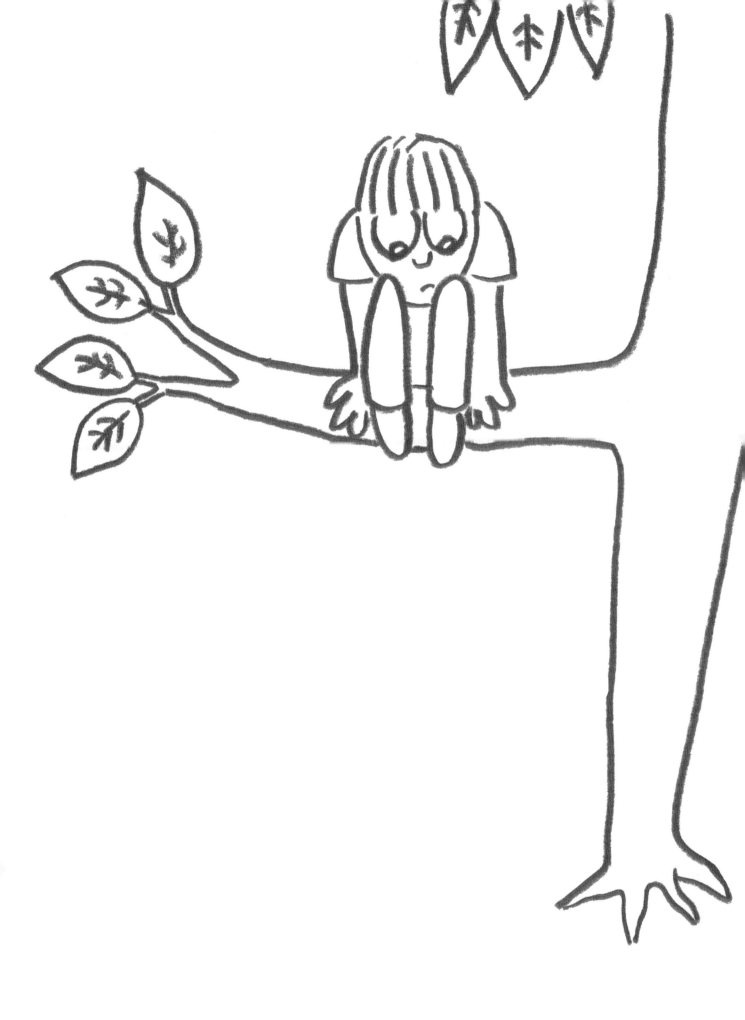

Help me get down.

Put some candles
on the cake.

What kind of eggs
are in the nest?

# What's that smell?

What's that noise?

# How much can you carry?

# Make a swarm.

# Pull me along.

Lift me up.

Charm the snakes
from the baskets.

What's in the web?

# Who's behind the bushes?

# Beware of the sea monster!

A can of worms.

Everything's topsy turvy.

# Make a loud BANG!

Hang up hats
and coats.

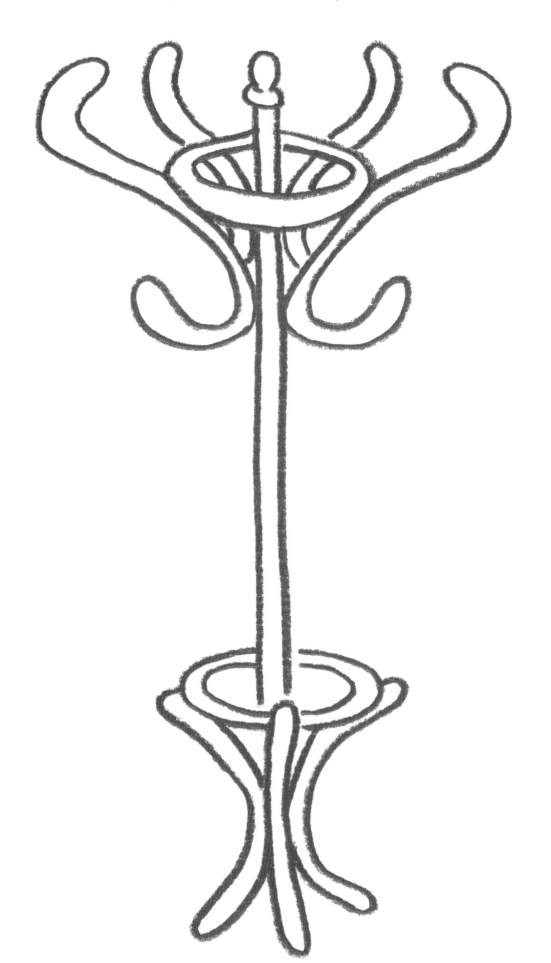

# Decorate the room for a party.

Fill the pot to
make a spell.

# What's in your stocking?

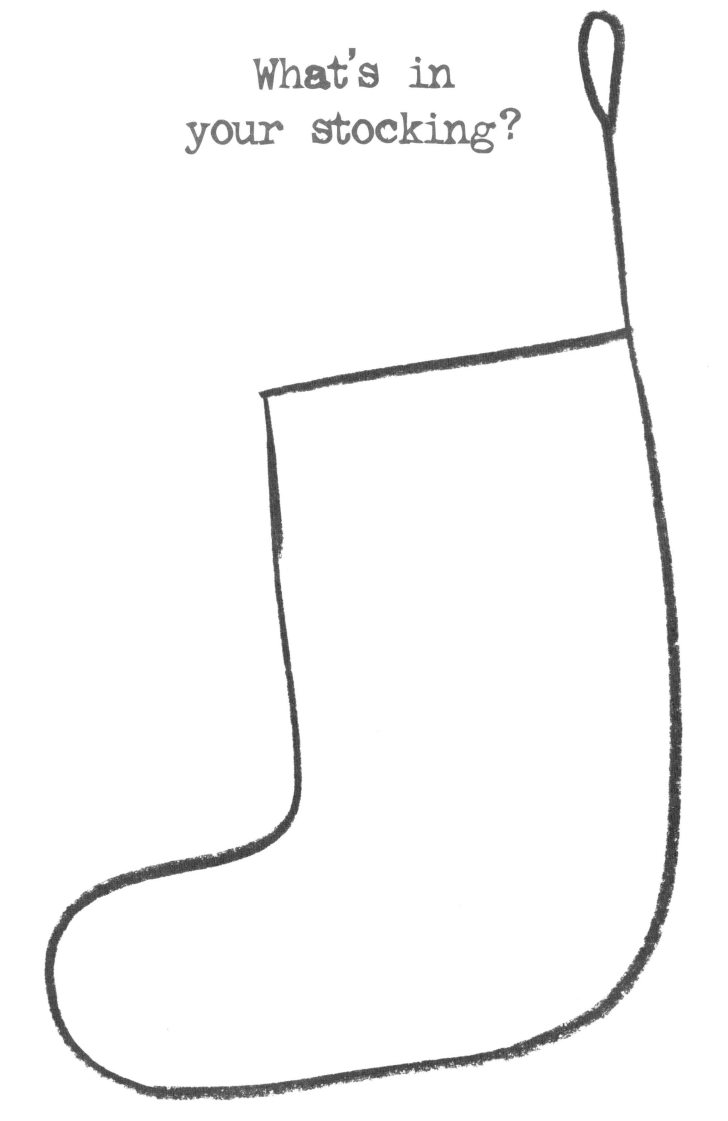

# Put some photos in your **album**.

# Make the drink fizzy.

# Create a crazy hairstyle.

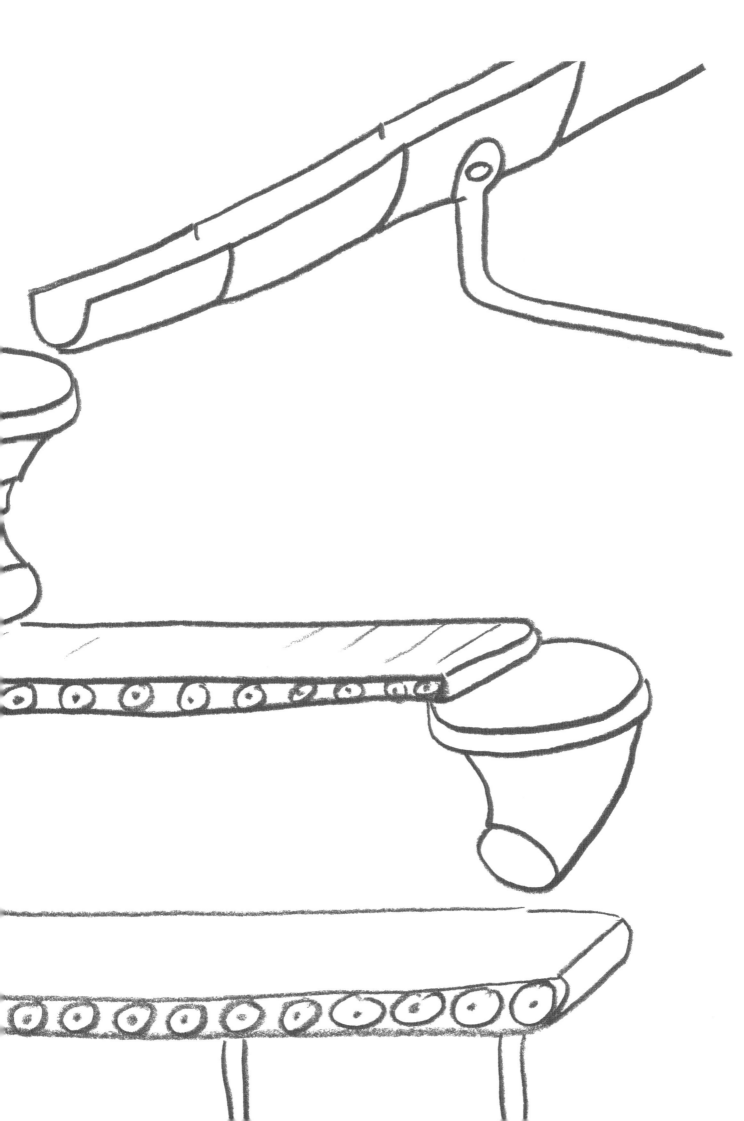

# What's inside?

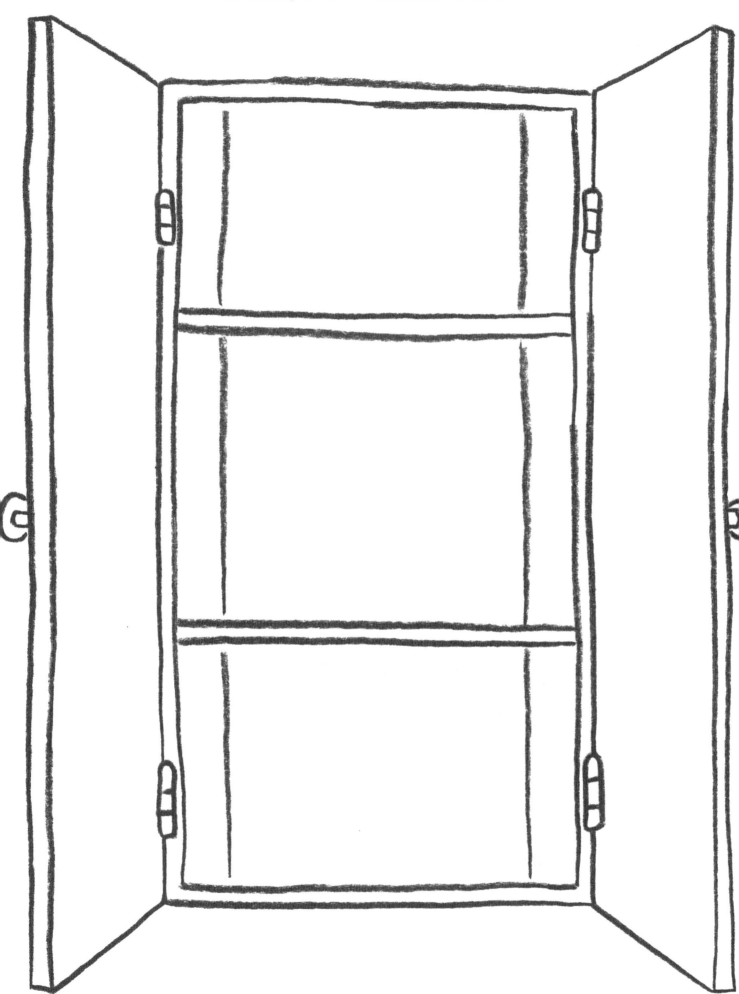

# Make a tasty dessert.

Put the vehicles on.

# What's on television?

# Wrap the presents.

# Who's in the field?

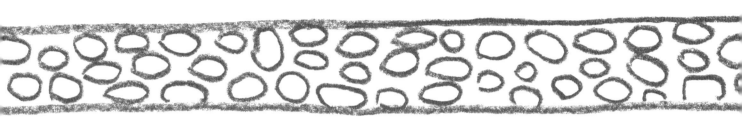

Build a wall.

# Decorate the egg.

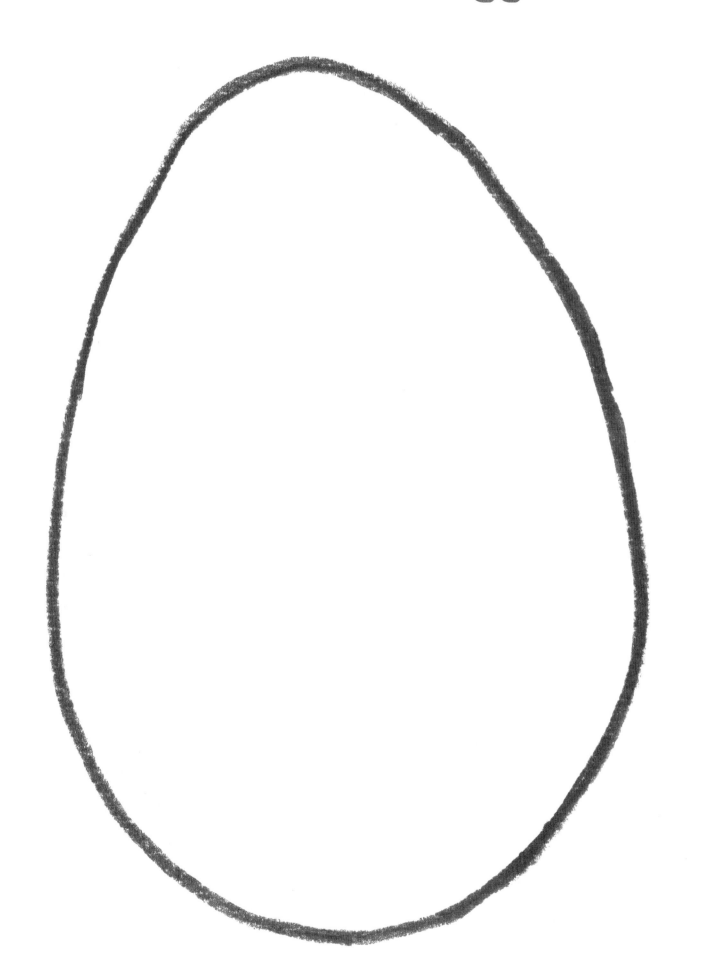

Is there a monster
under the bed?

# Whose noses?

# Put some holes
# in the cheese.

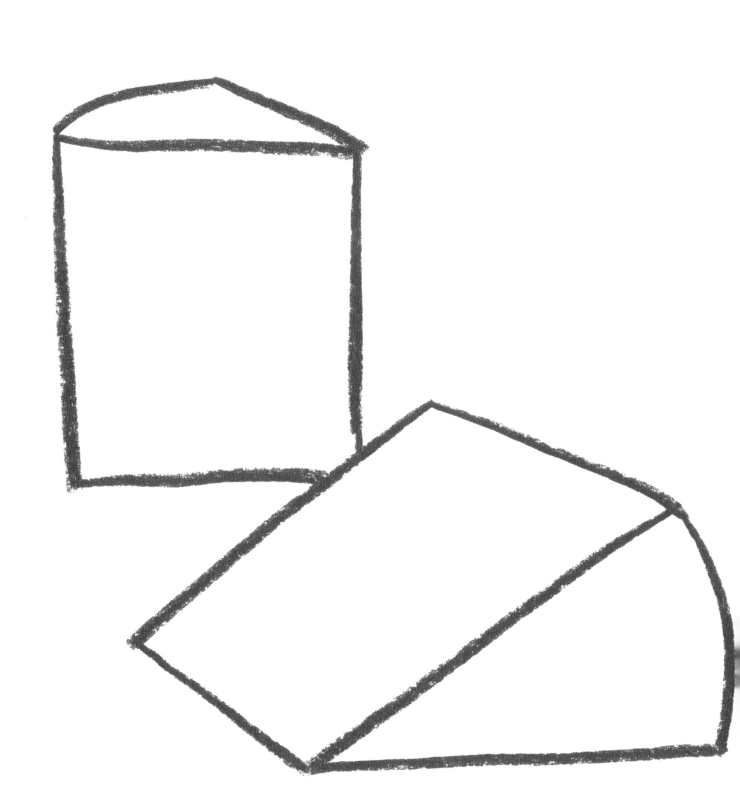

# What's in the secret hiding place?

I can see it!

What can you jump over?

# Design a T-shirt.

# What's in the wash?

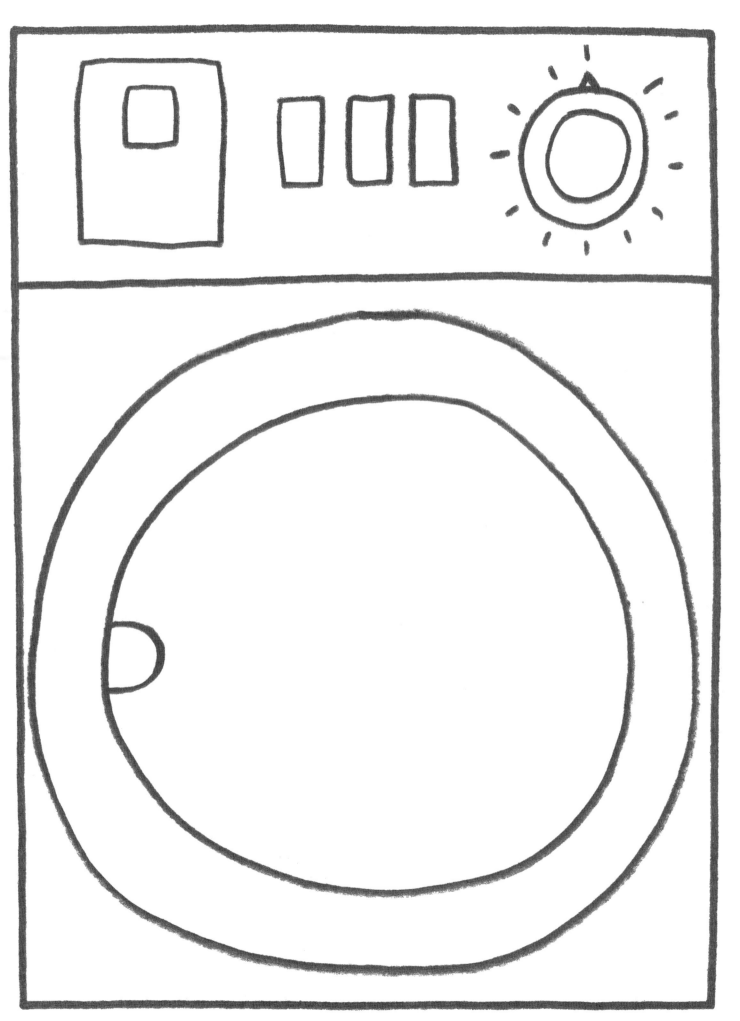

# Fill the jar with cookies.

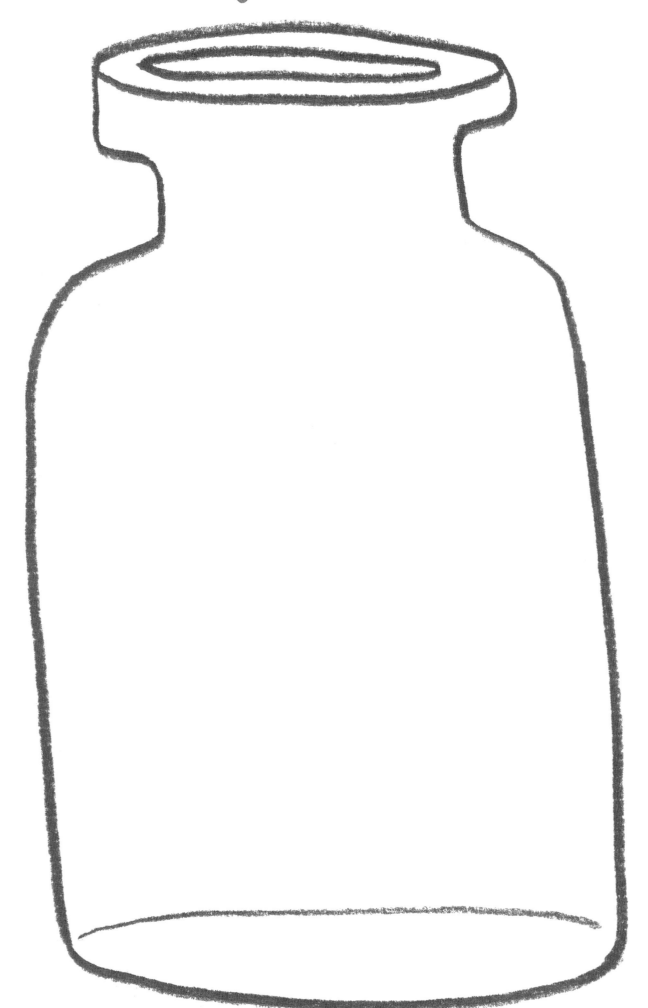

# Magnify the ants.

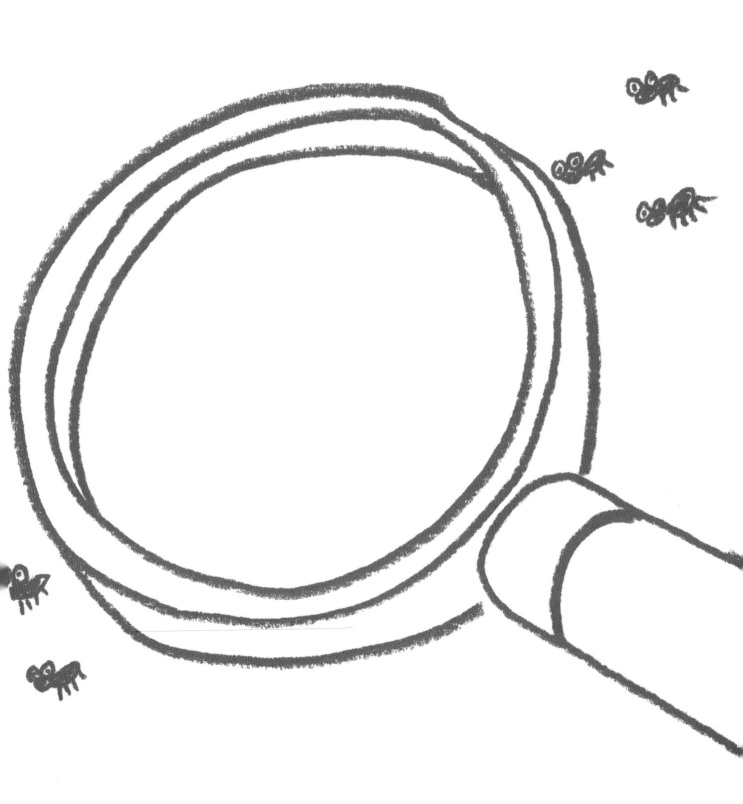

What's in my pouch?

What is the
birdwatcher watching?

# What do you see in the crystal ball?

Fill the box with anything you want.

Balance something on
the seal's nose.

# Put legs and wings on the insects.

What goes under?

# What do you take to bed?

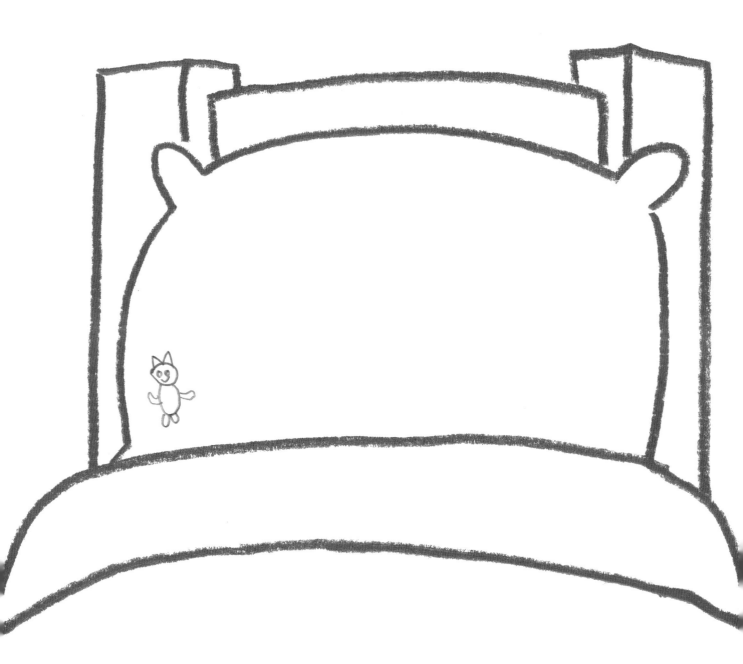

Give me
a tattoo.

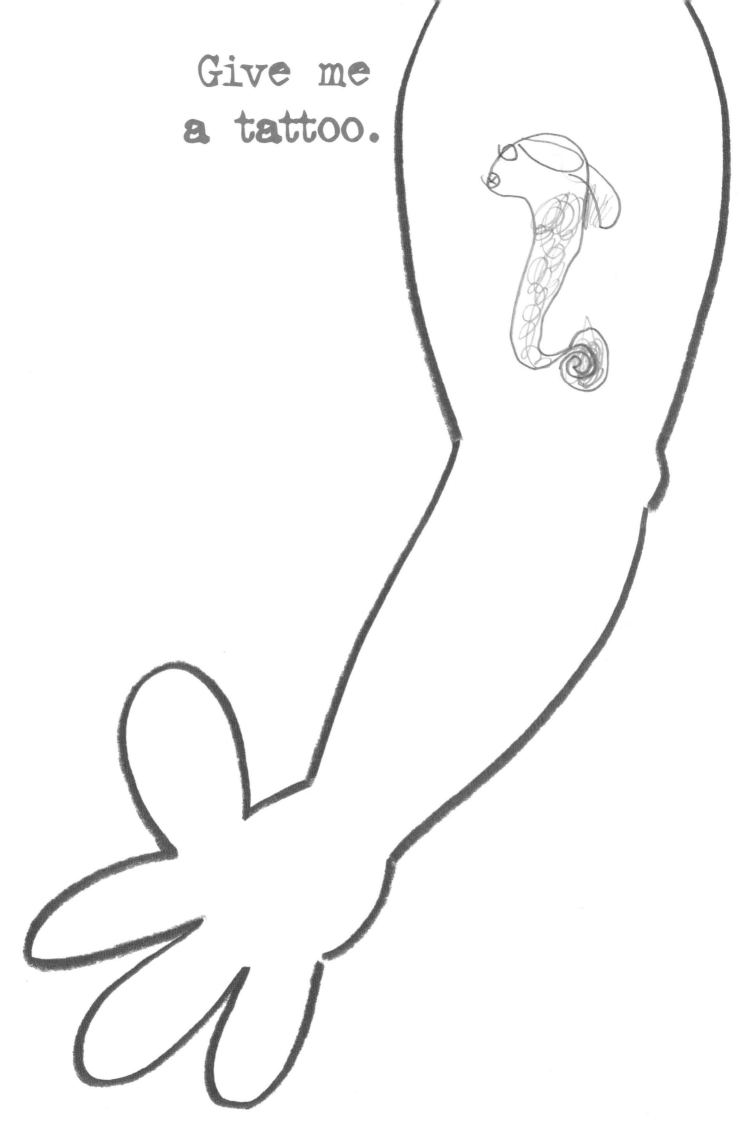

Any **alligators**
in the **swamp?**

The zebra and the
tiger need stripes.

# Give the pig **a mud bath.**

# What's in the attic?

# What are you scared of?

Finish the pattern.

Whose houses?

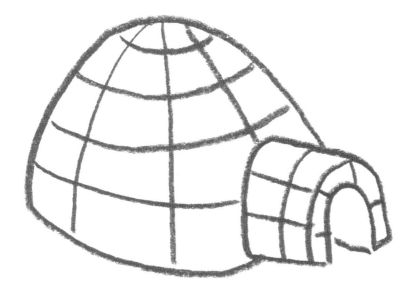

# What did they catch?

# What do caterpillars turn into?

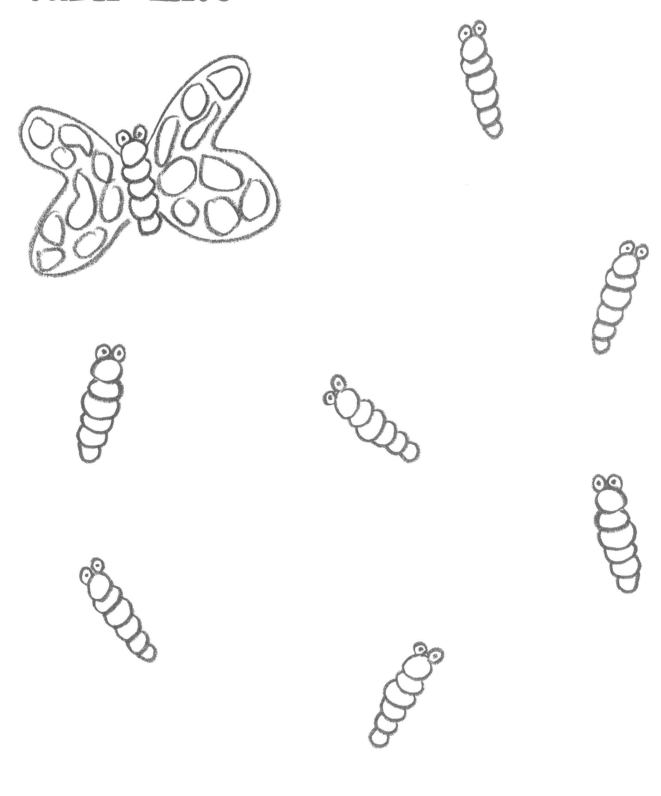

I'll huff **and** I'll puff ...

# What am I lifting?

Show my skeleton.

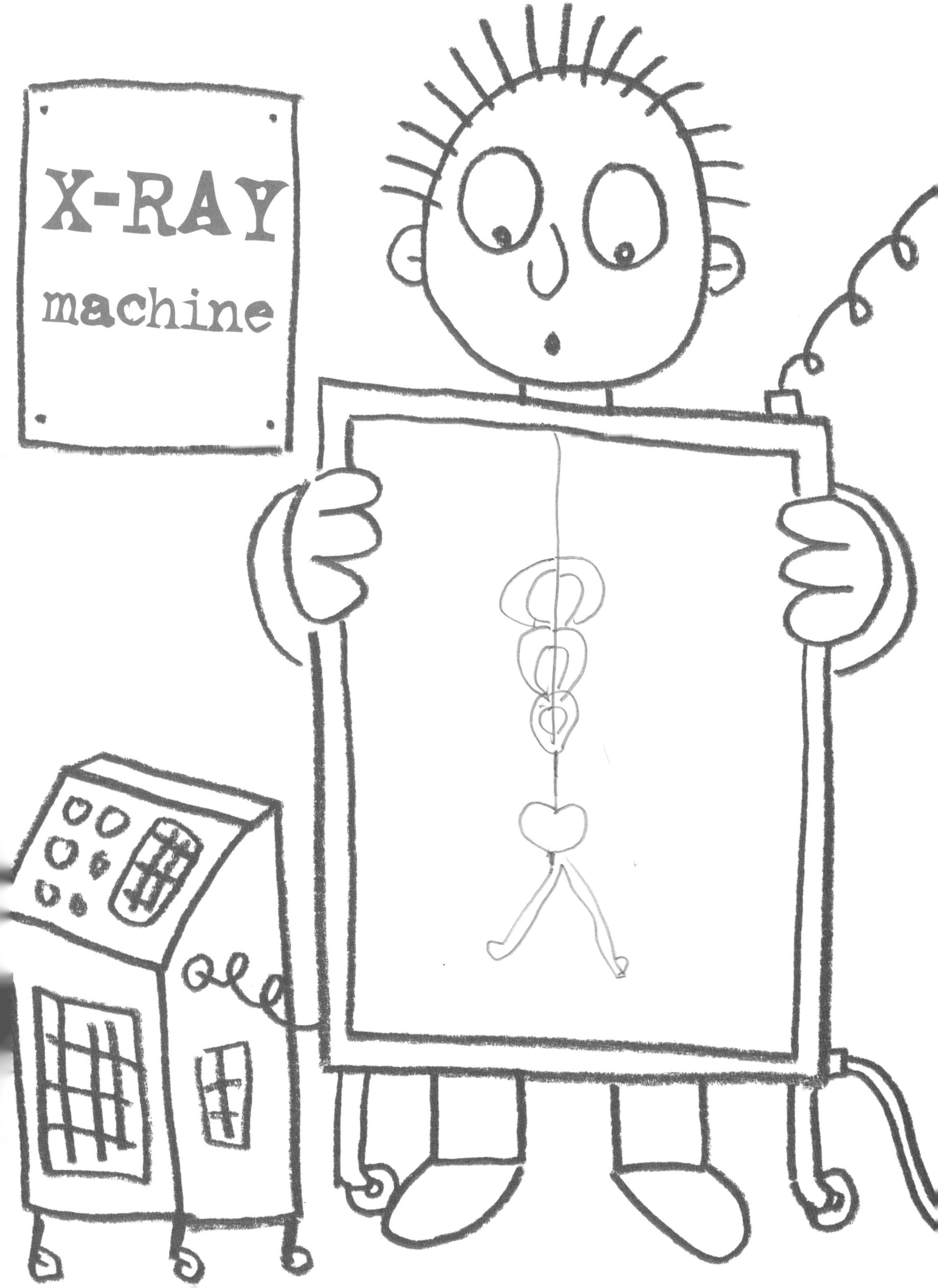

# Fly the kite.

# What is the cat chasing?

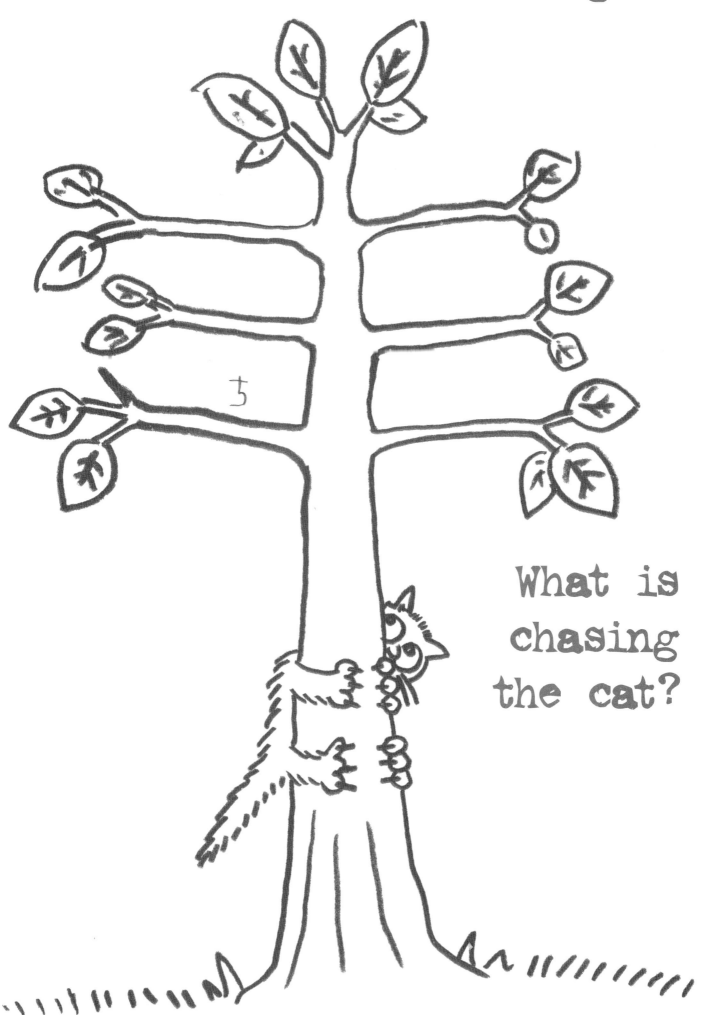

What is chasing the cat?

# What do you play with in the bathtub?

It's huge!

It's tiny!

# Whose teeth?

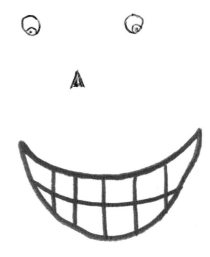

What are you playing?

# Open the box and let it loose!

# Attach some balloons.

# Build a treehouse.

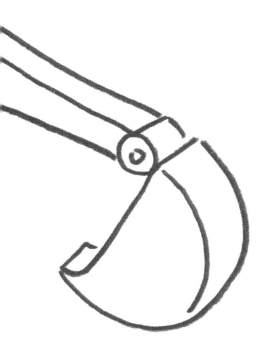

Dig a great big hole.

Finish the pattern.

# Set the table.

# Fill the bookshelves.

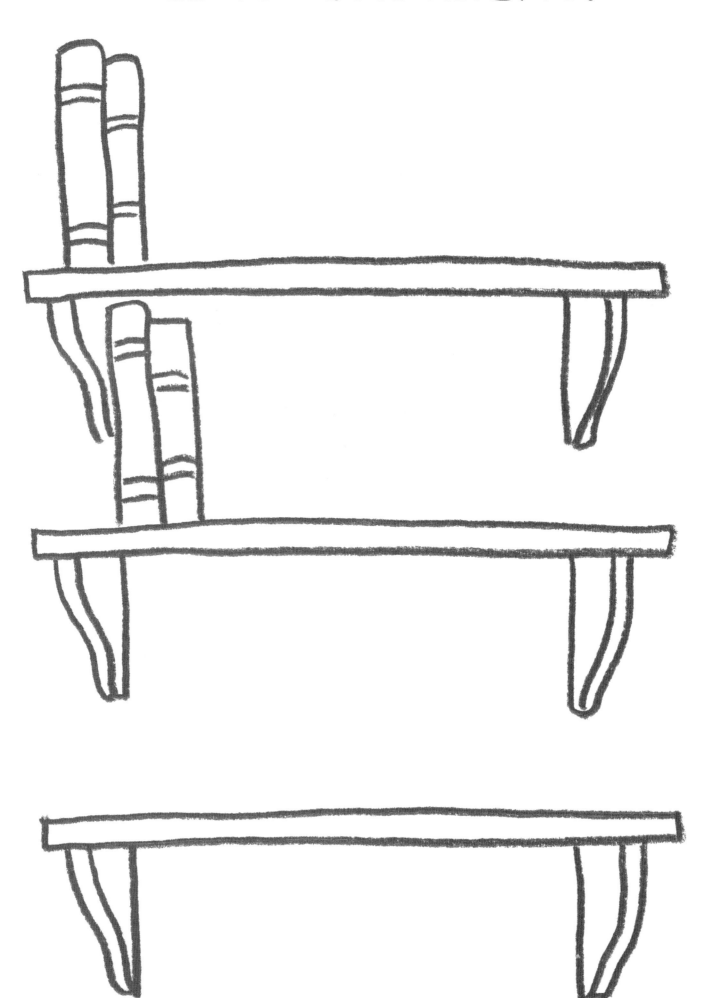

# Pin some medals on the General.

Who needs
glasses?

# Look what you did!

# What's under the rock?

Give the penguin some fish.

# Fill the chest with treasure.

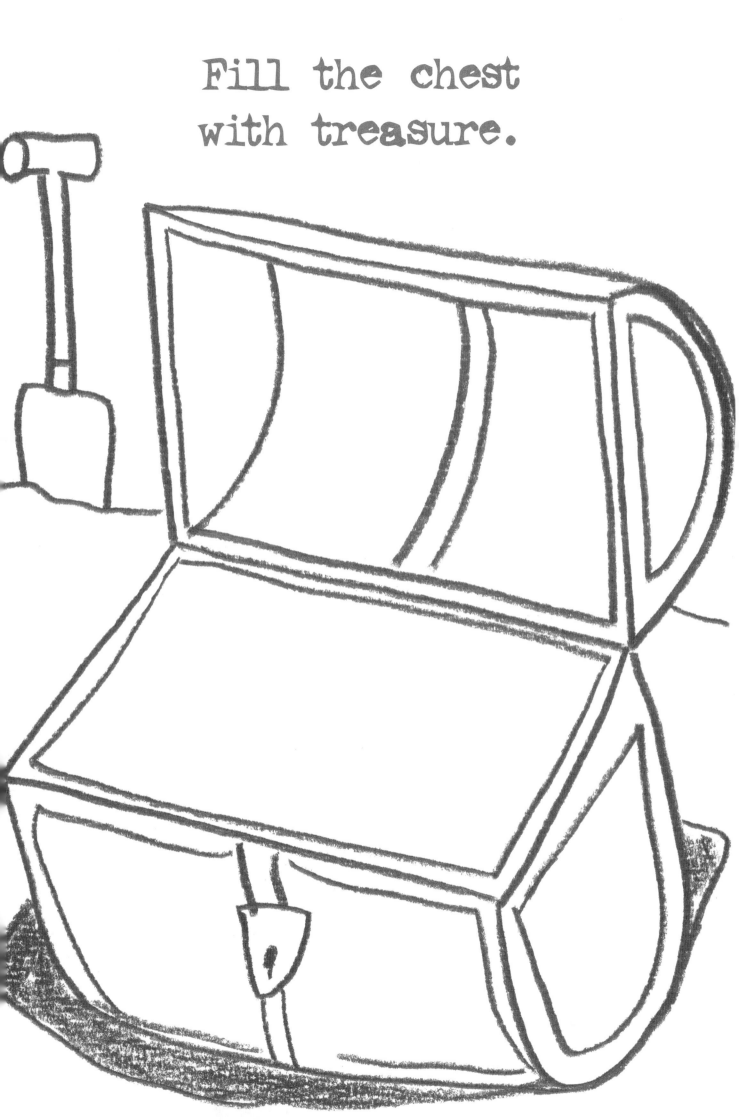

Make the sun shine.

# Shoot to score!

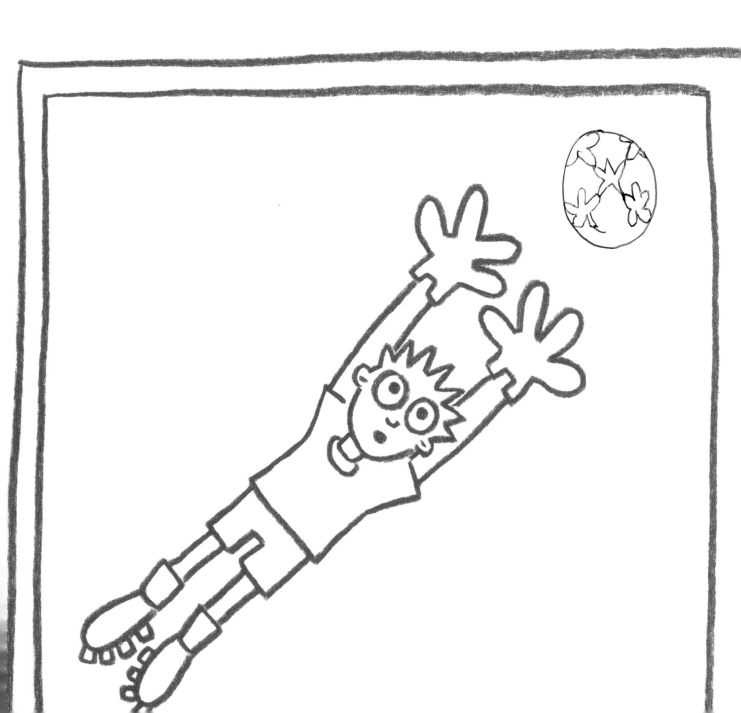

Show the reflection
in the lake.

# Make a masterpiece.

# What am I pushing?

There was an old lady
who swallowed a ...

# What's lighter than a feather?

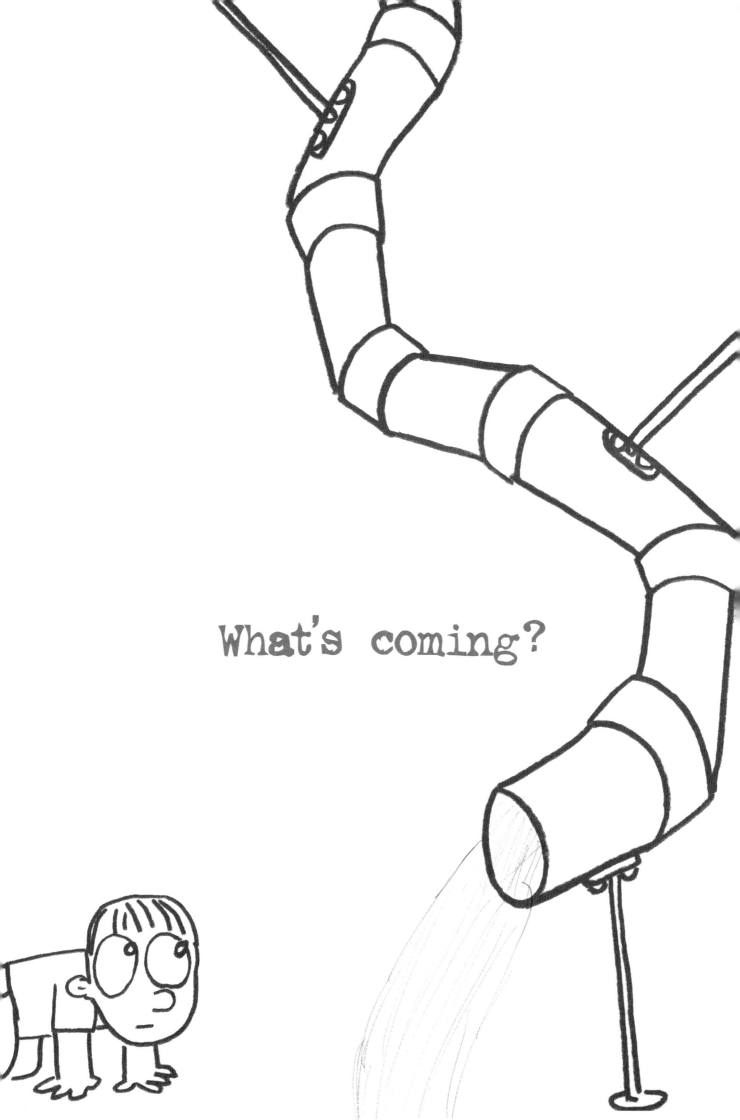

What's coming?

# What's heavier than an elephant?

# Hang out your washing.

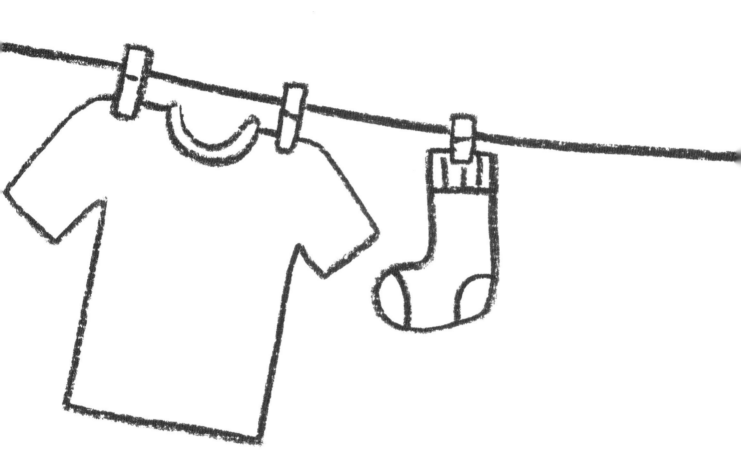

# What's for breakfast?

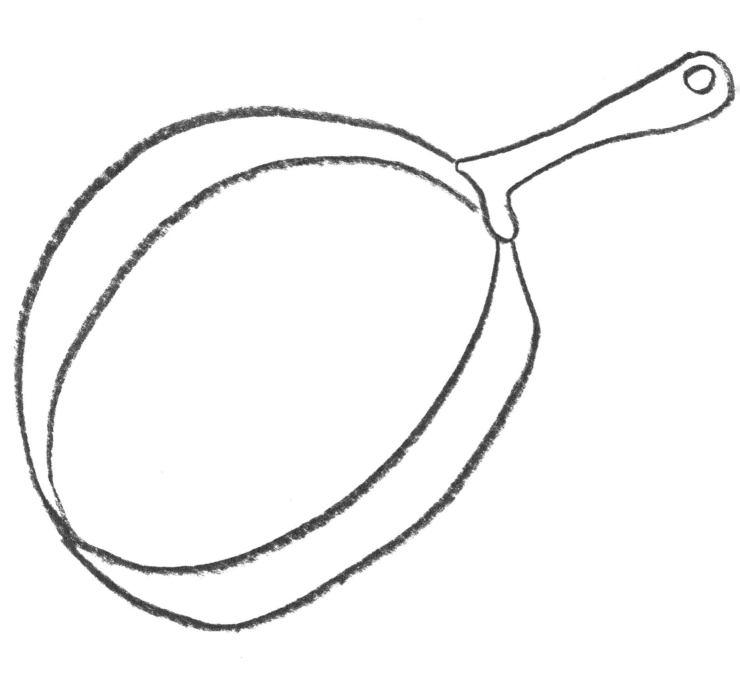

LOST

Make a thunderstorm.

# What's growing?

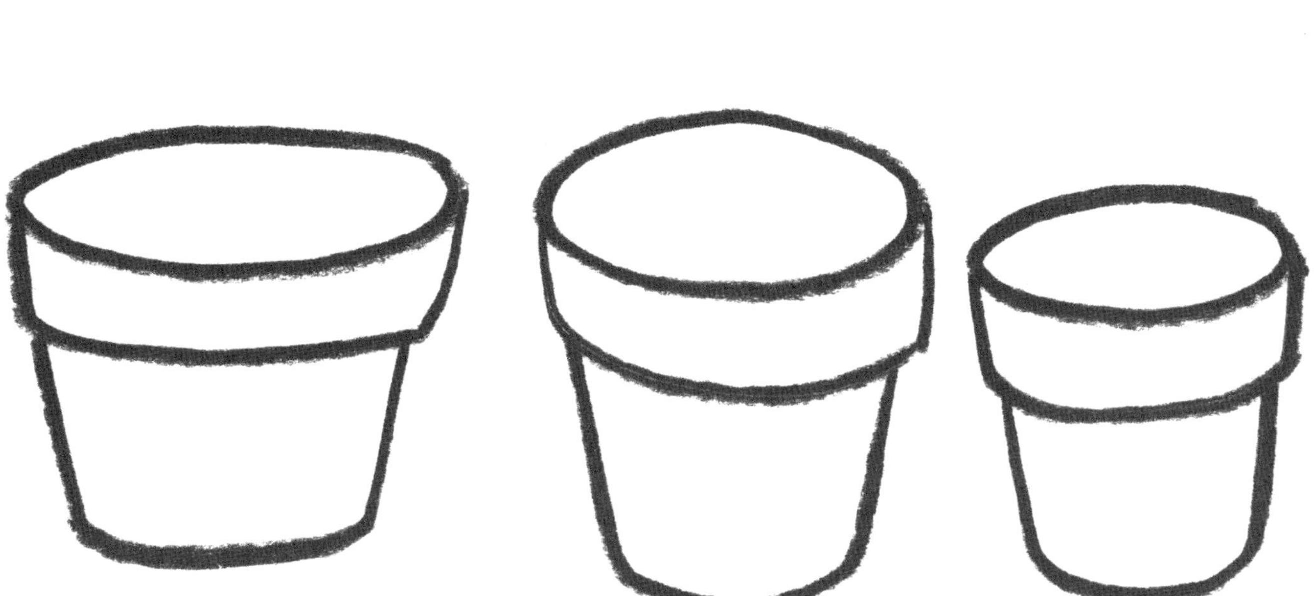

The cow jumped
over the moon.

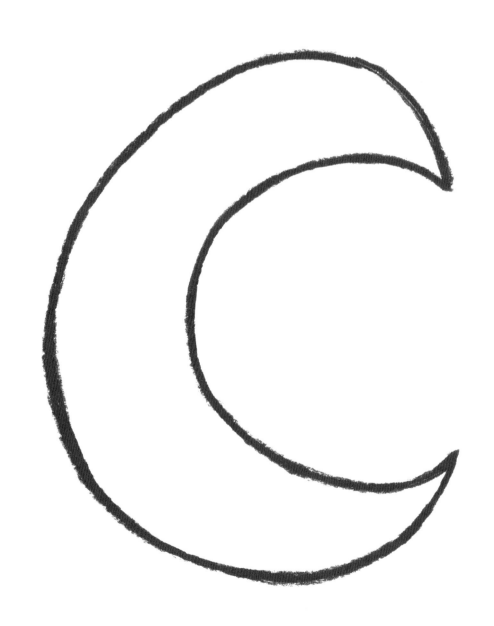

Show my reflection
in the mirror.

What's behind me?

# Who **are** you **ta**lking to?

Who walked where?

# How many can you juggle?

# What did you buy?

Give me some friends.

# Tickle me.

# What do monsters dream of?

# Fill the piggy bank with money.

Magic beanstalks.

# Give the birds a tree.

# Finish the pattern.

I spy with my little eye
something beginning with D.

# What do you wish for?

March them up to
the top of the hill.

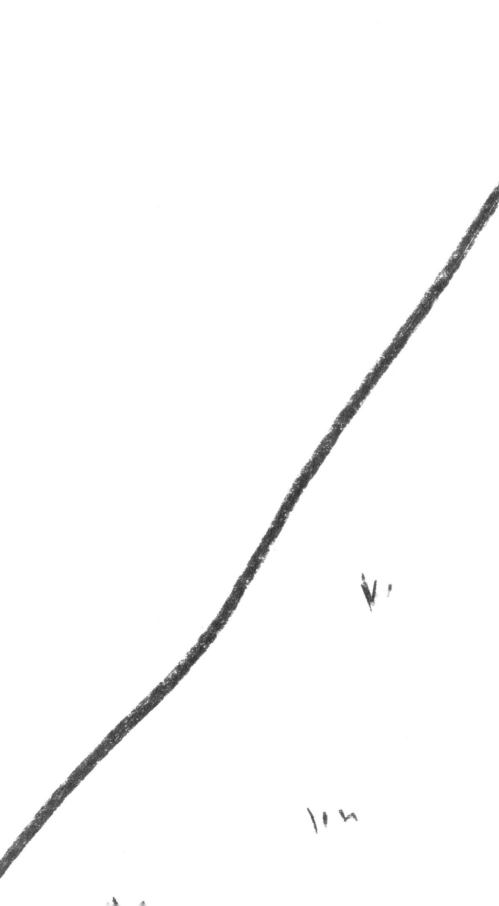

March them
down **again**.

# Build a robot.

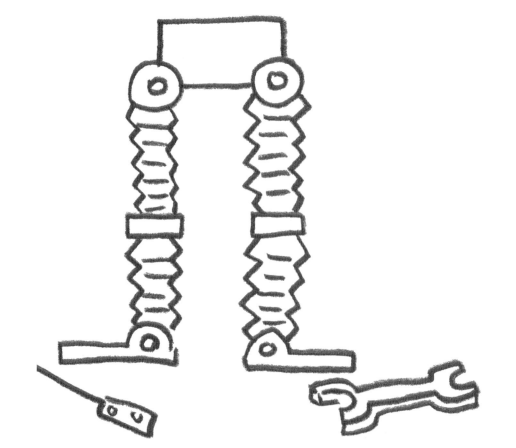

# What's on the other end?

TREASU

# Watch out for the octopus!

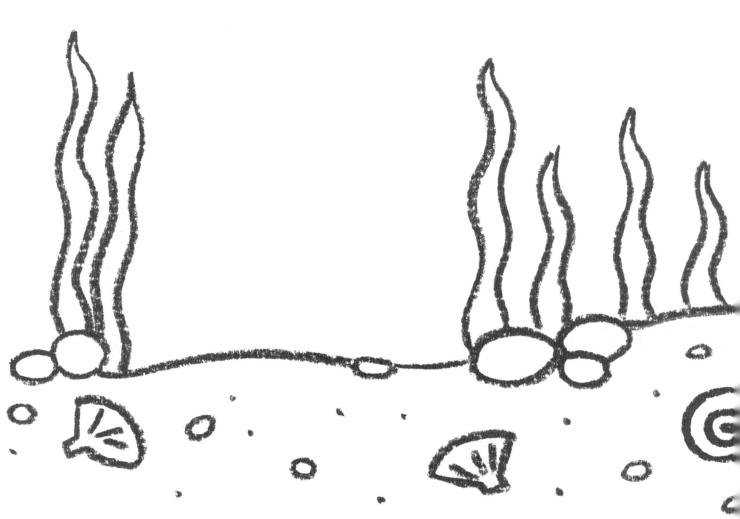

# Aliens have landed!

What's in the cages?

It's biting my foot!

Who's at the windows?

# Let them all loose!

# What's for sale?

# Who's at the door?

# What's taller than a giraffe?

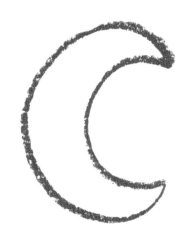

Put some stars in the sky.

# Any sharks in the water?

# Feed the animals.

# What pizza topping would you like?

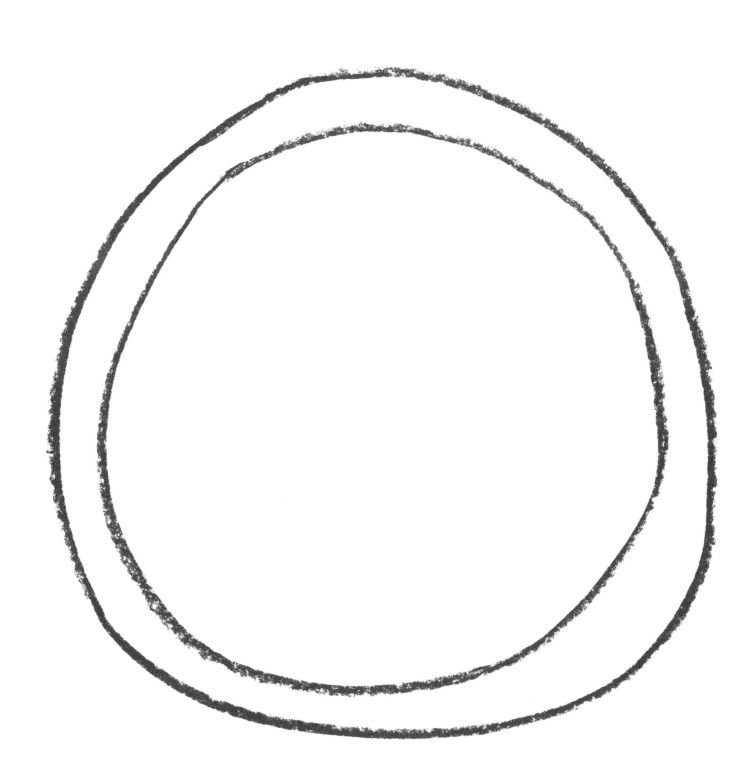

Design and lace
the shoe.

Stop the traffic.

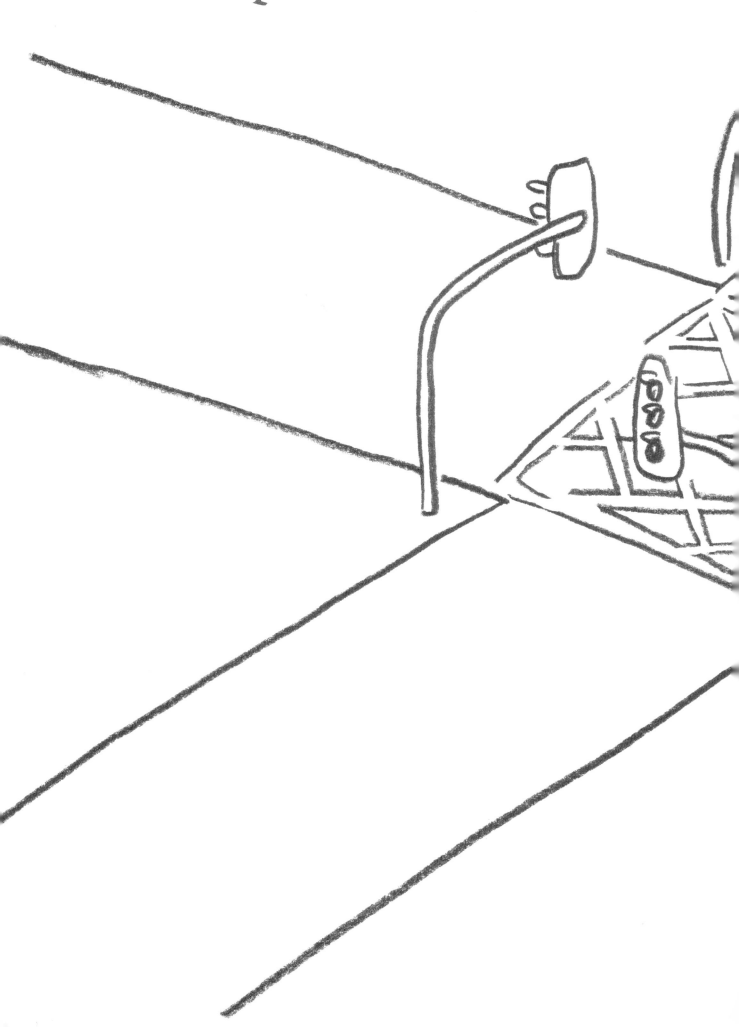

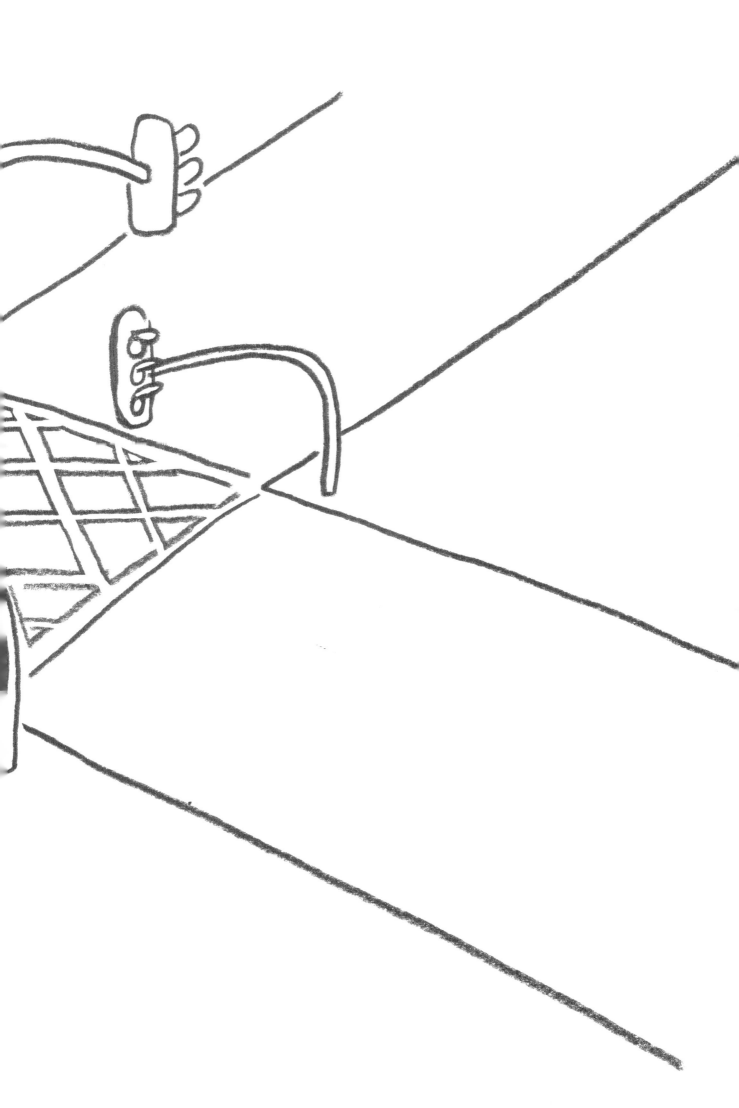

Build a sandcastle.

# Finish the pattern.

# Who's in the park?

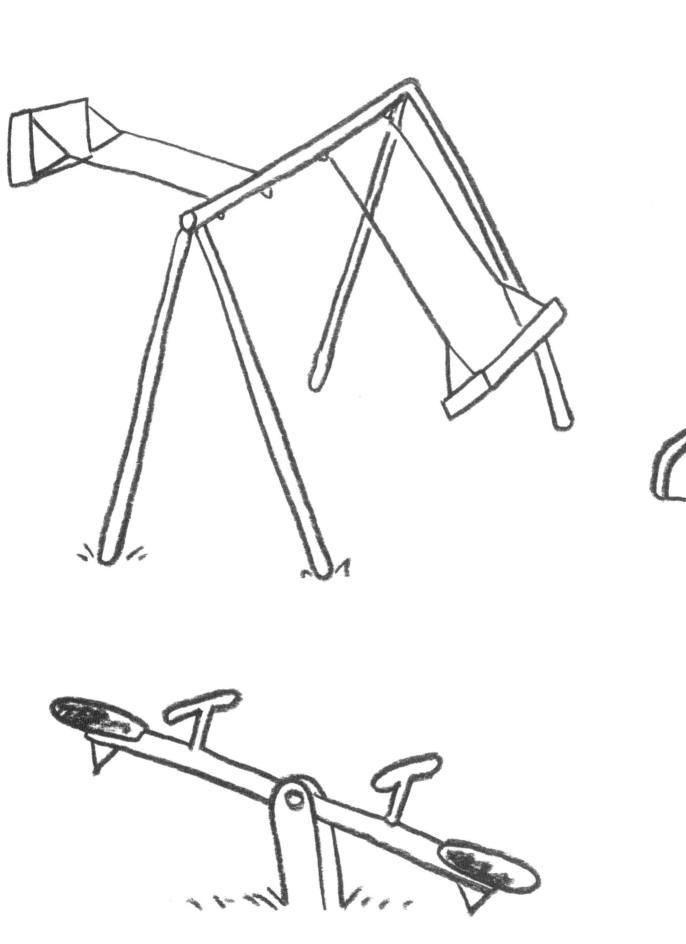

What would you invent?

Give the lady some jewels.

# Whose feet?

# Make a trap to catch the baddie.

Knit the world's
longest scarf.

# Complete the maze.

Who lives here?

# Finish building the city.

# What did the window cleaner see?

Dress the snowman
and woman.

# Ready for take off?

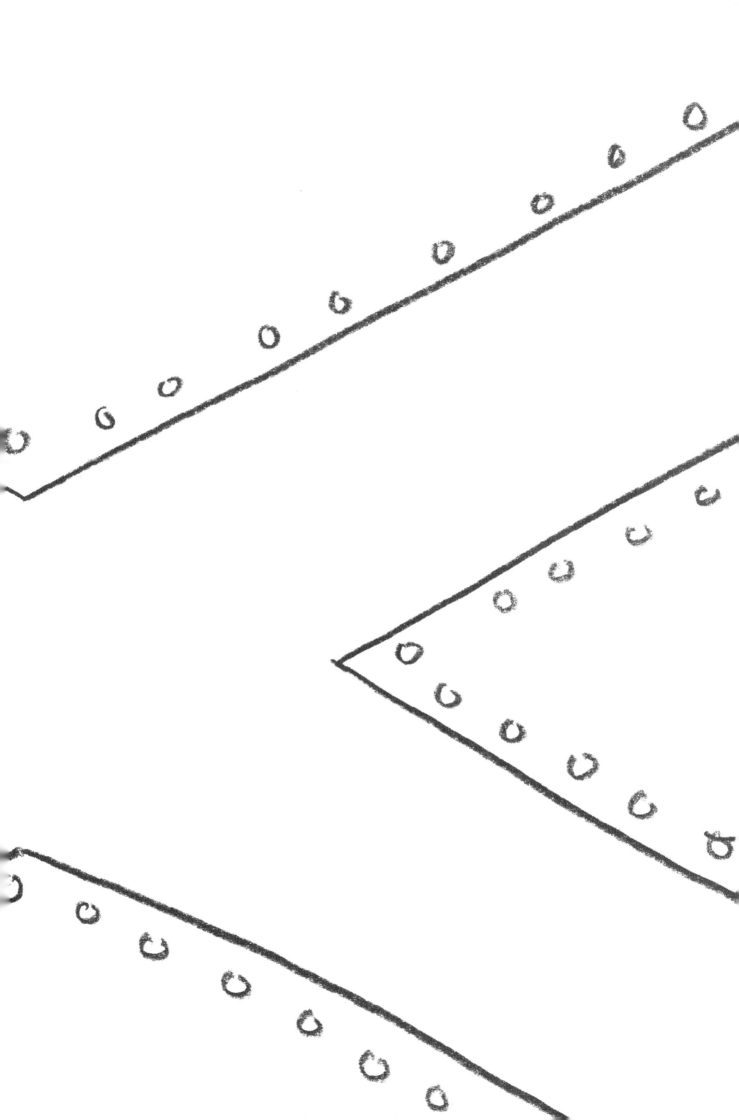

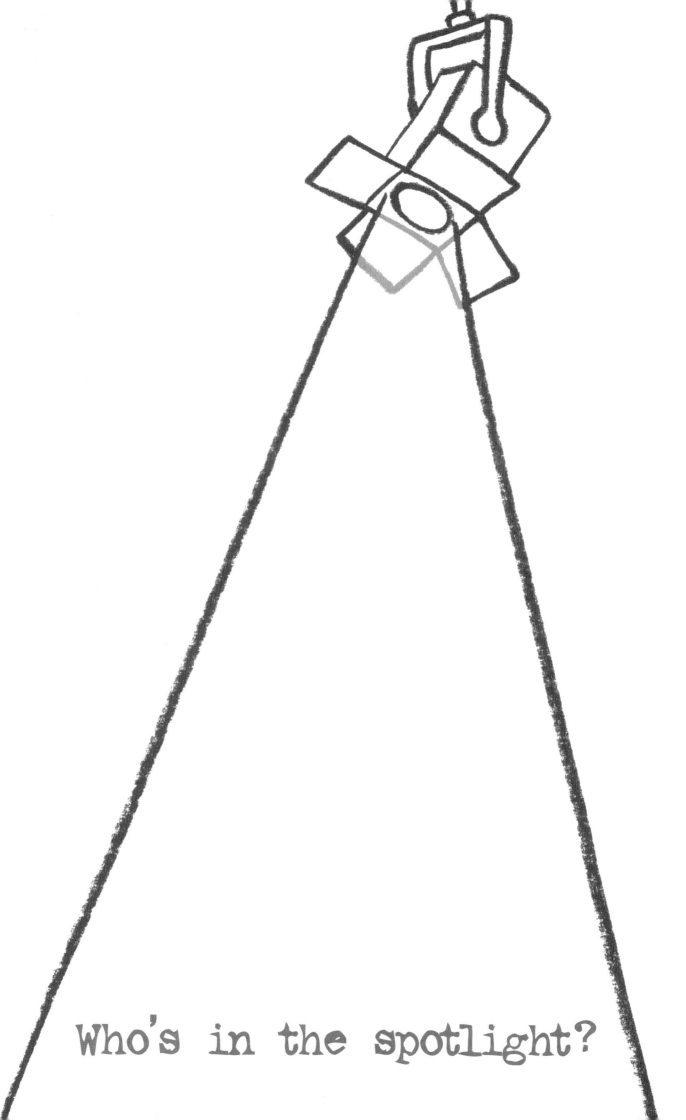

Who's in the spotlight?

Who's in the crowd?

What's in the basement?

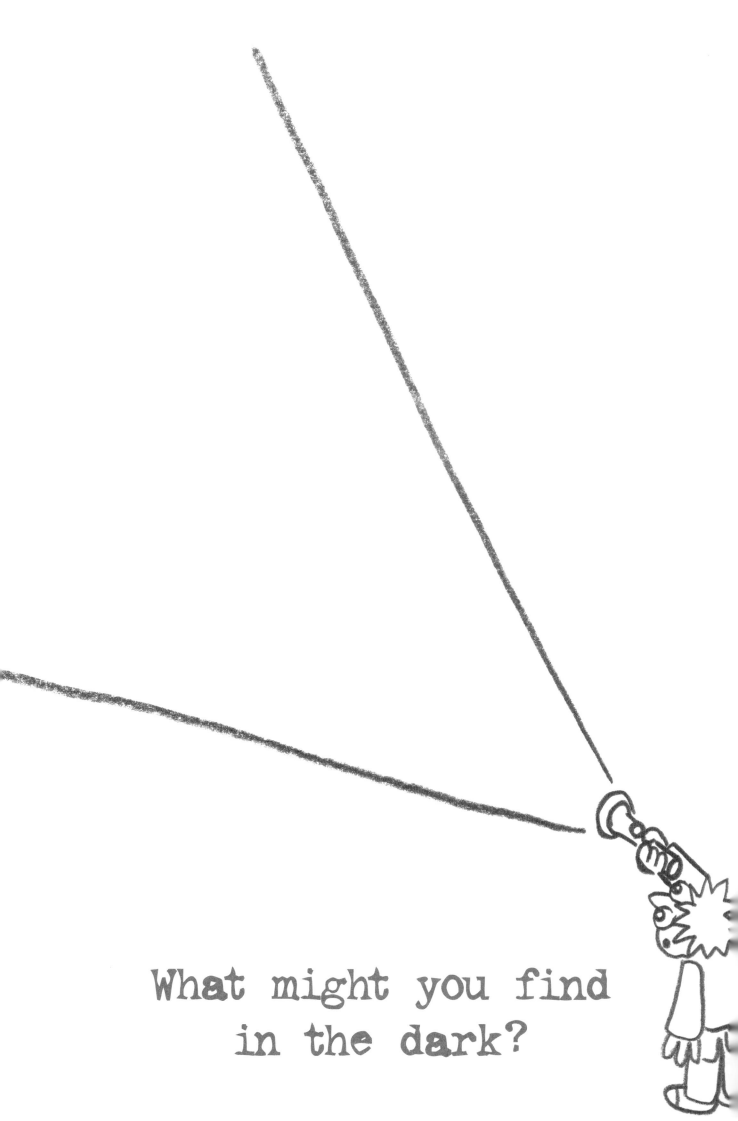

What might you find
in the dark?

# Where am I?

Win the race.

# Fill the bus.

# What's underground?

We're going to **a**
costume party.

# Whose hats?

# Decorate the tree.

That's a lovely present!

# Make a traffic jam.

Who's in
the jungle?

# Finish the pattern.

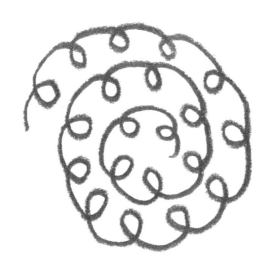

# Who's the champion?

# What can you see inside?

# What can you see outside?

# Where are we going?

# What has hatched?

# Do some tricks.

What's coming out
of the tunnel?

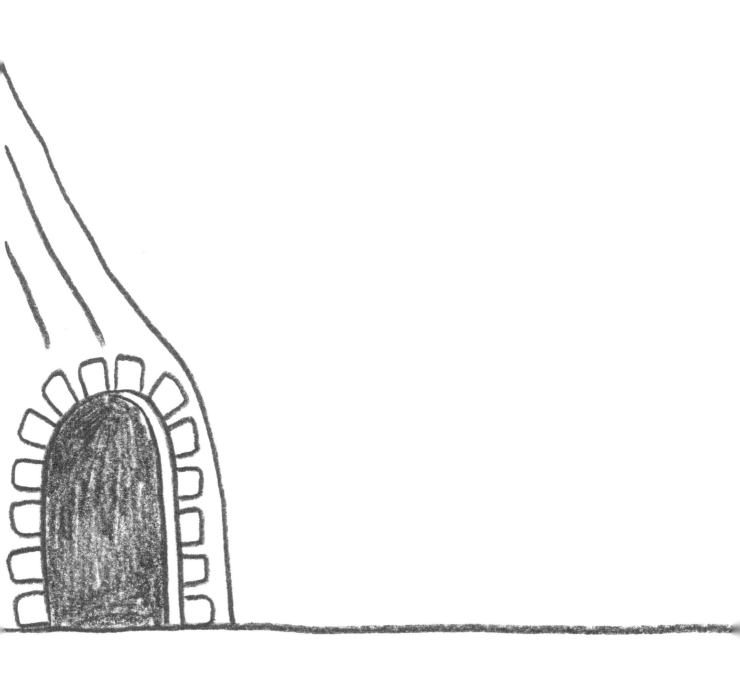

# Why did the chicken cross the road?

Walk the tightrope.

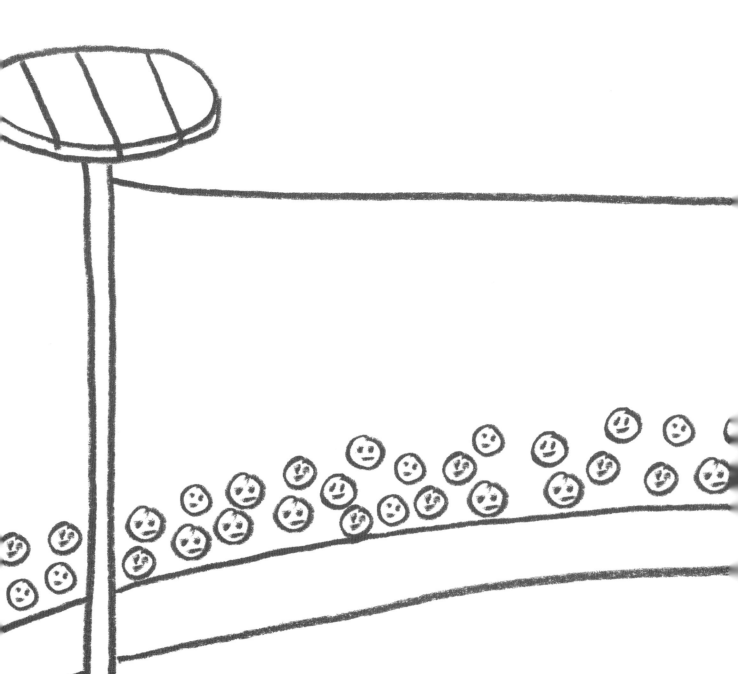

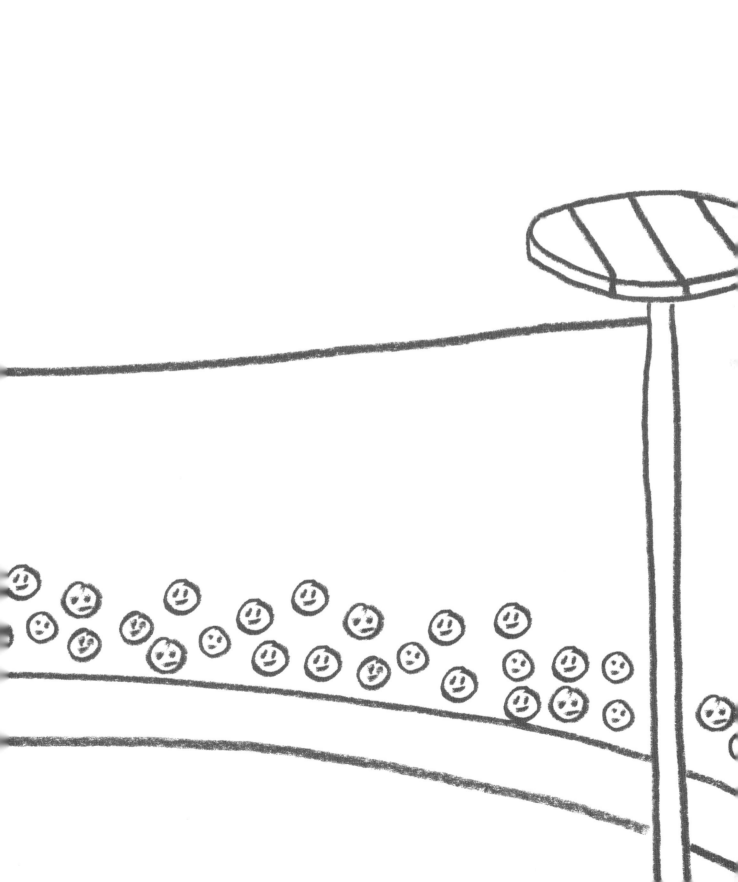

Here's a baby dinosaur.
But where's its daddy?

# WANTED